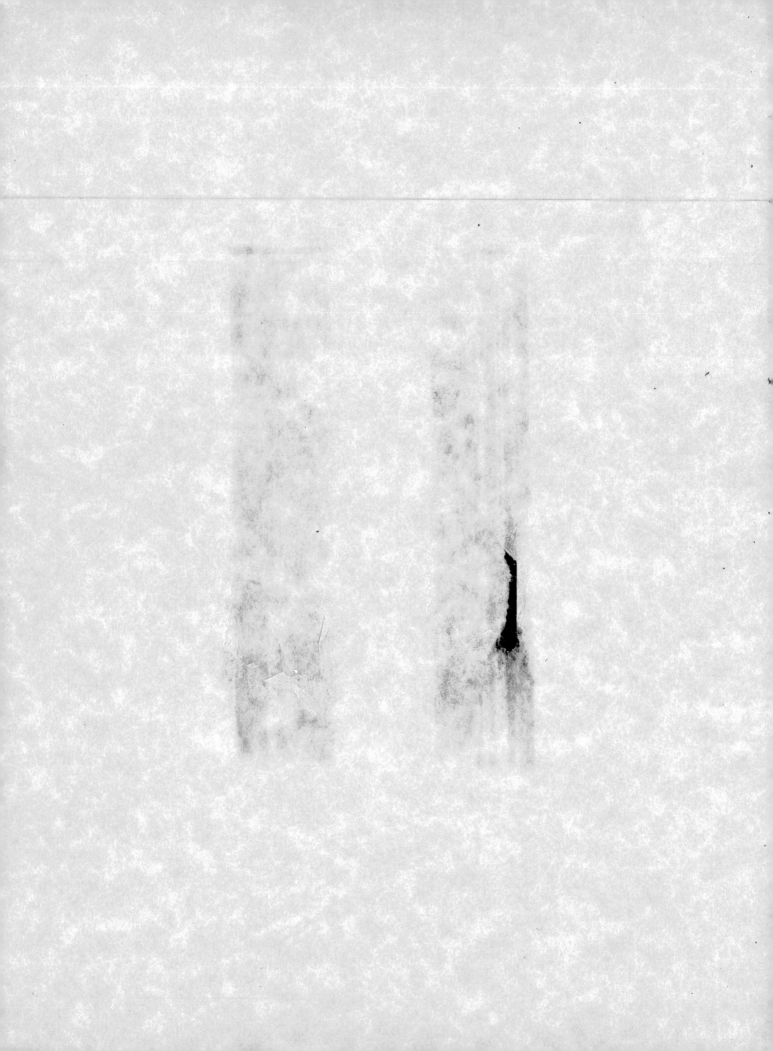

The American Revolution

EDWARD F. DOLAN

The American Revolution

HOW WE FOUGHT THE WAR OF INDEPENDENCE

THE   MILLBROOK   PRESS   •   Brookfield, Connecticut

Cover photo courtesy of Bettmann Archive

Photos courtesy of Bettmann Archive: pp. 13, 46, 76 (top), 80, 96, 100;
Library of Congress: pp. 14, 20, 22, 24, 26, 34, 37, 43, 45, 55, 59, 63, 74, 76
(bottom), 77, 81, 83, 84, 88, 94; National Archives: pp. 25, 29, 57, 71, 79;
North Wind Picture Archives: pp. 31, 33, 40, 41, 52, 65, 91.

Maps by Frank Senyk

Library of Congress Cataloging-in-Publication Data
Dolan, Edward F., 1924–
The American Revolution: how we fought the War of Independence /
by Edward F. Dolan.
p.   cm.
Includes bibliographical references (p.) and index
Summary: Describes the Revolutionary War, highlighting military
strategy, dramatic battles and leading figures of the rebellion.
ISBN 1-56294-521-1 (Lib. Bdg.)
1. United States—History—Revolution, 1775–1783—Juvenile
literature. [1. United States—History—Revolution, 1775–1783.]
I. Title.
E208.D655   1995
973.3—dc20   94-44440   CIP   AC

Published by The Millbrook Press, Inc.
2 Old New Milford Road
Brookfield, Connecticut 06804

Contents

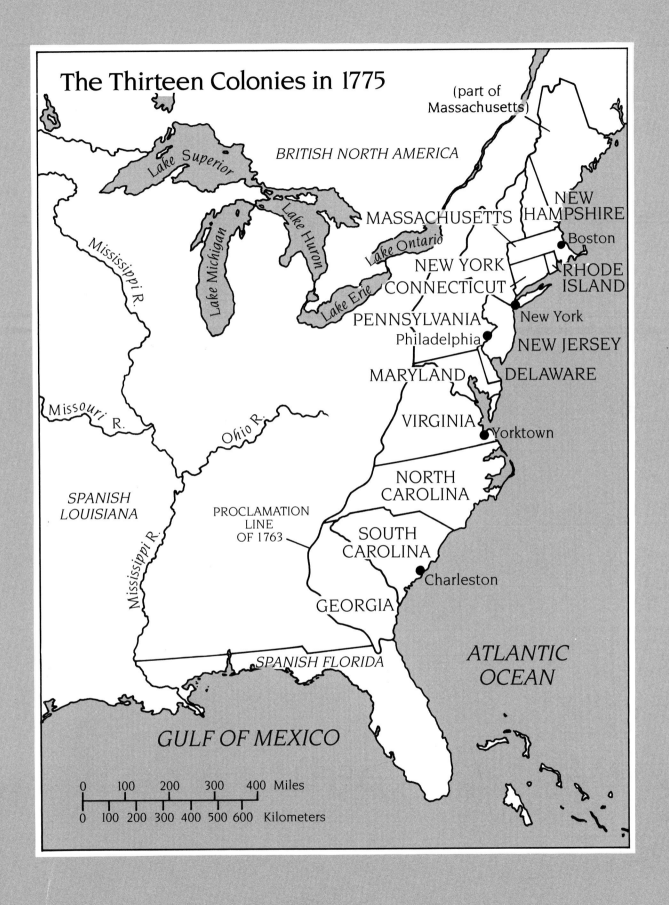

The Thirteen Colonies in 1775

(part of Massachusetts)

BRITISH NORTH AMERICA

Lake Superior

Lake Michigan

Lake Huron

Lake Ontario

Lake Erie

Mississippi R.

Missouri R.

Ohio R.

Mississippi R.

MASSACHUSETTS

NEW HAMPSHIRE

Boston

NEW YORK

CONNECTICUT

RHODE ISLAND

PENNSYLVANIA

New York

Philadelphia

NEW JERSEY

DELAWARE

MARYLAND

VIRGINIA

Yorktown

NORTH CAROLINA

SPANISH LOUISIANA

PROCLAMATION LINE OF 1763

SOUTH CAROLINA

Charleston

GEORGIA

SPANISH FLORIDA

ATLANTIC OCEAN

GULF OF MEXICO

| 0 | 100 | 200 | 300 | 400 Miles |

| 0 | 100 | 200 | 300 | 400 | 500 | 600 | Kilometers |

The American Revolution

CHAPTER 1

The Muskets of April 19

At sunrise on April 19, 1775, some seventy men, dressed in farm clothing and clutching muskets, stood on the village common at Lexington, Massachusetts. They stared at the road that ran past the common. Very soon, the hated British redcoats would come swinging along that road on their way to the little town of Concord 6 miles (nearly 10 kilometers) away. Then there could be gunfire and death.

The men knew that the coming meeting had been in the making for years—years that had seen England's thirteen American colonies endure an increasingly harsh rule by their mother country. The opposition to that rule had flamed hotter with each passing year, finally reaching such a heat that the people were ready to rebel. They had formed a citizen army of Minutemen, so called because they could take up arms against their oppressors at a moment's notice.

Here in the Massachusetts colony, the Minutemen had spent the past months storing military supplies at Concord. They knew that General Thomas Gage, the commander of the British forces at Boston, was aware of the cache. They were certain that one day he would send out troops to destroy it. That day was now dawning.

In Boston, some 20 miles (32 kilometers) away, a group of Americans had been watching for any move by Gage. Last night, they had sent two riders, Paul Revere and William Dawes, galloping across the countryside with word that Gage's troops were finally heading for Concord. The Minutemen had sprinted through the darkness to Lexington to intercept the British march.

Now, standing with their commanding officer, Captain John Parker, they heard the tramp of approaching feet. Moments later, six companies of light infantry swung into view, the cool sun glittering on their muskets. At their head rode Major John Pitcairn.

Parker heard a groan when his Minutemen saw how greatly the Britishers outnumbered them, and he told them to stand their ground. Next, he heard Pitcairn order the soldiers—they were called redcoats because of their scarlet jackets—to form a battle line. The troops broke ranks and spread out along the edge of the common, yelling as they ran.

Pitcairn galloped to the front of his troops. Like General Gage in Boston, he did not want a fight that would lead to bloody warfare. He wanted only to reach Concord and cripple the rebellious colonists by destroying their military cache. He called for the Americans to lay down their arms and disperse.

Staring at the troops, Captain Parker realized how hopeless the situation was. He responded to Pitcairn's order by telling his men to disband but to keep their muskets. The Minutemen turned to leave the common. A fight was on the verge of being avoided.

Paul Revere

When Revere rode out with the warning that the British were marching on Concord, he was captured by a British mounted patrol. His warning was then spread through the countryside by other riders. Revere was a talented silver-smith and a dedicated patriot who participated in a number of rebellious actions prior to the war, among them the Boston Tea Party.

Paul Revere warns of the British approach.

A handful of Minutemen faced a much larger British force on Lexington's village green. When the first shot rang out, the Revolutionary War began.

But, abruptly, shots rang out. No one ever knew whether they came from the common or from Minutemen concealed behind a nearby rock wall. Whatever the case, a red-coated soldier toppled and Pitcairn's horse reeled as two musket balls struck it.

Somewhere in the British ranks, an officer screamed the order to open fire. Muskets erupted all along the redcoat line. Eight Americans died instantly. Ten fell wounded and began staggering away to safety.

Pitcairn cursed at the tragic turn of events. With his horse plunging beneath him, he shouted for his men to do no more than surround and disarm the Americans. But the soldiers were in no mood to listen. They were exhausted and angry. They had been marching all night. And they had endured the hostility of the Massachusetts people for months. They wanted revenge. Their muskets went on crashing as they ran forward with fixed bayonets.

By now, all the surviving Minutemen but one, Jonas Parker, had left the common. Wounded and bleeding, he stood alone, trying to reload his musket. The British bayonets swept in on him. Seconds later, he lay dead.

The deadly meeting had lasted mere minutes. Pitcairn stared at the common with regret and began reassembling his troops. They had been serving as an advance unit and, as they were re-forming, the main body of the British force arrived. Leading on horseback was the commander of the march, Lieutenant Colonel Francis Smith. In all, he had between 600 and 800 soldiers under his command. He ordered them on to Concord.

THE BATTLE AT CONCORD

Waiting at Concord were about 400 Minutemen from the town itself and the surrounding countryside. On gathering the night before, most had rushed to the home of their commander, Colonel James Barrett, a short distance away. Certain that the British knew it was serving as the rebels' military storehouse, they had hauled away its contents—muskets, powder, and musket balls—and had hidden them in the nearby woods.

At mid-morning, the Minutemen lay concealed in the hilly woods around the town. Silently, they watched Smith's troops enter Concord. Smith immediately sent four companies off to Barrett's house. Their path took them across the North Bridge, which spanned the Concord River just outside town. Three companies followed them to guard the bridge on its Concord side. Up on the wooded hill beyond the wooden crossing, Colonel Barrett and his men kept a watchful eye on the activity below.

Inside Concord, the redcoats searched the homes for hidden arms. In one building, they found sacks containing 500 pounds (227 kilograms) of musket balls and threw them into a millpond. Next, they came upon several gun carriages and set them afire, an act that triggered a battle out at the North Bridge.

The distant smoke from the burning carriages caught Colonel Barrett's eye. He had wanted to avoid a battle with the crack British troops if possible, but now ordered his men to save the town but not to fire unless fired upon. The Minutemen started down the hill to the North Bridge. Leading them were Captain Isaac Davis and little drummer boy Abner Hosmer.

The troops at the bridge stiffened at the sight of the advance. Then, as the Americans drew closer, the redcoats opened fire. Their first shots fell short. Seconds later, their targets came within range. There was a second burst. Captain Davis and Abner Hosmer dropped with fatal wounds.

Horrified on seeing the two drop, the Minutemen spread out and returned the fire. Nine redcoats fell wounded. Three were killed. Within minutes, the British were ordered to withdraw. They retreated—moving so quickly that they left their dead and wounded behind.

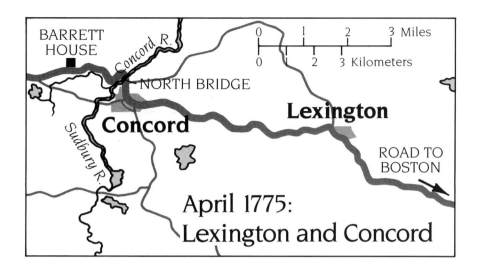

April 1775:
Lexington and Concord

The Minutemen surged across the bridge in triumph. But suddenly they broke off their pursuit of the fleeing troops. Perhaps because they did not want to meet the main British force, they stopped and then ran back to their positions up among the trees. Some paused to carry away the bodies of Davis and Hosmer.

Soon they heard the sound of marching feet coming from the direction of Barrett's home. They watched a line of sullen redcoats move past after finding nothing there. And they watched as the soldiers, staring in shock, stopped to remove their wounded and dead comrades who lay on the bridge. Then the soldiers disappeared from view.

In town, Lieutenant Colonel Smith assembled all his troops. By now, it was noon. Carrying his wounded and dead in carriages, he headed back to Boston.

———

The fighting at Concord was at an end. But after years of colonial anger with British rule, the American War of Independence—the Revolutionary War—had begun.

The Roots
of Revolution

The roots of the Revolutionary War began to take shape long before that fateful April 19, 1775.

The roots were present in the nature of the people who first settled the wilderness that was to become the thirteen British colonies in America. They were an independent-minded people who were willing to risk the dangerous voyage across the windswept Atlantic because they wanted a better and freer life. Then their sense of independence—and that of their descendants—grew as they carved out homes in the New World and harvested their own food.

But despite their sense of independence, they had no thoughts of breaking away from their mother country. They were loyal to their king and proud of being British. England helped matters by allowing them to govern themselves and develop industries that could provide wares for domestic and foreign trade—industries such as tobacco farming, and timber cutting for home and ship construction.

But then, beginning in 1651, the British government stung the colonists with a series of laws called the Navigation Acts. With these measures, England sought to profit from the growing American trade. One, for example, demanded that all goods headed to the colonies from foreign nations had to pass first through English ports so that Britain could collect customs fees (fees charged to the countries sending the goods) on them. Another prohibited the Americans from shipping certain goods to any country but England because they were needed there.

England viewed the Acts as fair because they were in keeping with a commercial theory that was practiced by all the European countries with overseas possessions: mercantilism. The theory held that the colonies existed solely for the economic benefit of the mother country.

The Navigation Acts angered colonial America by restricting its overseas trade. But they did not trigger a fiery outrage because they were not strongly enforced by Britain. The Americans, with some growing rich in the process, simply smuggled their wares overseas.

And so, while there was some colonial discontent, the rage that eventually led to revolution did not come until the end of the French and Indian War in the mid-1700s.

NEW ANGERS

Throughout the 1700s, England, France, and Spain engaged in a series of wars in both Europe and America. In part, the fighting was aimed at deciding which of the three would become the dominant colonial power in the New World.

One conflict, the French and Indian War (so called because the surrounding Indian tribes joined one side or the other), erupted in 1754 when troops from French-held Canada marched south and laid claim to the giant Ohio Valley. The move shocked the British colonials because they felt that the valley belonged to them. The result: nine years of fighting that saw the invaders ousted and France made to surrender Canada and other areas to the British.

Though victorious, England was left heavily in debt by the costs of the war. And so, since the mother country had battled to protect the colonies, the newly crowned King George III said the colonies should pay for the

A cartoon published in the *Pennsylvania Gazette* in 1754 urged the colonies to unite. It appeared with an article by Benjamin Franklin promoting his Albany Plan for a central colonial government. The plan was rejected by Britain, but it marked an early step toward unity.

fighting. He also felt that his country's rule over the colonies had always been too lenient and needed to be stiffened to reap a greater profit for England. Consequently, he and his Parliament took a series of disturbing steps.

First, he demanded that the Navigation Acts be strictly enforced. British warships swept the Atlantic, stopped all American vessels, and searched them for contraband cargo, causing the smuggling trade to suffer. On land, officers of the Crown broke into homes and went looking for smuggled goods without proper search warrants. The colonials charged that the privacy of their homes was being violated.

At the same time, King George and his Parliament ordered the colonies to pay tariffs on an increasing number of imported goods. Next, he called for a 10,000-man British army to be stationed permanently in America, announcing that the troops were meant to protect the people against Indian attack. The colonists were sure that the soldiers' real job was to see that the new tariffs were collected. The arriving red-coated troops were met with open hostility.

Then came the Stamp Act of 1765. It required the Americans to purchase government stamps to be placed on all legal documents, bonds, newspapers, insurance policies, and even playing cards. The colonists flew into a fresh rage. The recent tariffs were known as indirect taxes because they were aimed at businesses. But this was a *direct* tax on the people. They shouted that the king had no right to tax them directly because they were not represented in the British Parliament. Two organizations, the Committees of Correspondence and the Sons of Liberty, took shape throughout the colonies to oppose the Stamp Act. The Committees spread the news of what was hap-

King George III

George III, who ruled from 1760 until his death in 1820, ranks as Britain's longest-reigning male monarch. Despite stern measures that he and his Parliament directed against the American colonies, he was considered a good king who sought to put an end to the corruption in his country's politics. He suffered a metabolic disorder that finally cost him his sanity and his sight.

pening in each colony because of the Act. The Sons of Liberty made their opposition known through speeches and noisy street demonstrations. So great was the ire that the Stamp Act was repealed a year later.

But King George soon devised a fresh set of hated laws. They began with the Quartering Act of 1765, which called for the colonials to make room in inns and other buildings for the arriving redcoats. A second act, in 1774, required them to put the redcoats up in their homes. The Americans, growling that their privacy was again being violated, refused to admit the soldiers.

They growled even louder when new tariffs were next set on imported glass, lead, paper, and tea. The people retaliated by boycotting (refusing to buy) these items. Everywhere there was discontent. Street disturbances, led by the Sons of Liberty, erupted in several cities.

A "MASSACRE," A "TEA PARTY," AND THE "INTOLERABLE ACTS"

The disturbances led to tragedy on March 5, 1770, when a group of Boston citizens taunted and threatened a sentry outside the Customs House. A shouting crowd gathered and troops were summoned to restore quiet. The Bostonians greeted them with a hail of snowballs and rocks. Angered, the soldiers loosed a volley of musket fire into the crowd. Eleven people fell to the ground; five dying. The incident was dramatically christened the "Boston Massacre" and added fire to the colonial anger.

For months, Britain had recognized that the new tariffs were harming its colonial trade. On the very day of the Boston Massacre, the government repealed all the

The Boston Massacre fueled resentment against the British.

tariffs except the one on tea. King George stubbornly clung to it to show that he would not bend to the Americans.

The move quieted matters for a time. Then tempers flared again in 1773, when a fleet of tea-laden ships sailed into various colonial ports. The Maryland colonists set fire to one ship and destroyed it. In New York and Philadelphia, angry mobs kept the tea crates from being unloaded.

The harshest reception was given to the three ships that anchored at Boston. Late one night, a group of townsmen donned Indian garb, rowed out to the vessels, and clambered aboard. Whooping wildly, they hauled 342 tea crates up from the holds and heaved them overboard.

Nicknamed the "Boston Tea Party," the attack triggered a greater wrath than ever in King George. He demanded the cantankerous Americans be brought under control once and for all. As punishment, Parliament enacted a string of laws that colonials quickly dubbed the "Intolerable Acts"—and for good reason.

Although Patriots disguised themselves as Indians to dump tea into Boston Harbor, the event was not secret: Supporters cheered from the wharf.

A British cartoon shows leering Boston Patriots tarring and feathering a royal tax collector, while others dump tea into Boston Harbor.

One of the new laws closed Boston to sea trade until the people paid for the destroyed tea. Another of the Intolerable Acts took away the right of Massachusetts to govern itself and placed the colony under the rule of the British army.

In response to the Acts, delegates from the colonies met in Philadelphia in 1774 for what became known as the First Continental Congress. They discussed their complaints and then issued a Declaration of Colonial Rights and Grievances. In it, they held that the right to levy taxes belonged to them and petitioned the king to correct the wrongs being done to the colonies. The Declaration was politely worded because the delegates, despite their anger, were still loyal to the mother country. The king ignored their plea.

For many Americans, this was the final insult. The anger was at its greatest in Massachusetts. Its people were an especially independent lot and had always fiercely opposed the British laws. They had been among the first colonists to form Minuteman troops as the troubles with England began to threaten the possibility of warfare. Now, with the king's snub, the Minutemen began storing arms at Concord.

War with the mother country no longer seemed just a possibility but almost a certainty. However, though angry, many Americans did not want a complete break with Britain and the birth of a new nation. What they were ready to fight for was the granting of the rights that belonged to them as English subjects.

Then came that April day in 1775.

From Concord to Bunker Hill

When the British troops left Concord at noon on April 19, they were exhausted. They had marched all the night before. They had tasted battle and death. But now, heading back to Boston, they thought their troubles would soon be over.

They were wrong. The hundreds of Minutemen who had assembled the night before now dogged their every step. Darting among the trees alongside the road, the Americans sniped at the redcoats throughout the miles to Boston. One after another, soldiers toppled in the dust. The British fired back with their muskets and even their cannons. Enraged, they burned houses and barns alongside the road. They charged into the woods and fought the Minutemen hand-to-hand. At one spot, a group of redcoats chased twelve snipers into a home and bayoneted them to death.

Not until nightfall did the fighting end. The Minutemen faded away in the dark. The British column reached Boston with nearly three hundred dead and wounded comrades.

Marching back from Concord in tight formation, British troops were ambushed by rebels concealed in the woods along the road.

THE FLAMES OF REVOLUTION

Word of the Concord victory swept through the colonies. Everyone soon learned that the British had failed to destroy the arms cache and, as a result, had failed to take the fight out of feisty Massachusetts. Some colonies, still loyal to the Crown and wanting a peaceful solution to their problems with England, had opposed revolution. But now that the fighting had started, the leaders of all the colonies began to unite behind Massachusetts.

In the next weeks, the British commander, General Thomas Gage, saw Minutemen and ordinary citizens arrive from all the colonies and take up positions just outside Boston as if planning to attack and capture the city. But, once in place, they did not move. Armed with little more than muskets, they had not yet the strength for the task. Nor did Gage send out a force to drive them off. Rather, he asked England for reinforcements. He would fight back when they arrived.

THE SECOND CONTINENTAL CONGRESS

On May 10, 1775, while Gage was biding his time, the Second Continental Congress met at Philadelphia. Though some members still wanted a friendly settlement with Britain, the delegates spent little time talking about peace. They realized that the colonies must now fight for their rights.

They began by establishing the Continental Army and choosing the officer who would lead it. Several men who had fought in the French and Indian War were considered. In the end, the job went to one of the most respected of their number—the tall, forty-three-year-old Virginia planter, George Washington.

Washington accepted the post and said he would take command of the American troops at Boston as soon as possible.

George Washington

A tall Virginia planter (he stood over 6 feet 2 inches, or about 190 centimeters), Washington commanded the Continental Army throughout the war, though two of his generals—Charles Lee and Horatio Gates—tried to overturn him and take his place. Both failed in their attempts. Washington went on to become the nation's first president. Prior to assuming the presidency, he played an influential role in the 1787 Philadelphia convention that developed the United States Constitution.

George Washington in 1775.

THE BATTLE OF BUNKER HILL

General Gage's reinforcements arrived in June and brought the strength of his army to 6,500 men. Washington had yet to appear in Boston, and the British general now acted on a plan that had been on his mind for weeks.

The plan called for a British force to move north across the Charles River from Boston to the small peninsula where the village of Charlestown lay. Looming alongside the village was Breed's Hill and, just behind it, Bunker Hill. Both gave a commanding view of Boston. Anyone who held the two could rain shells in on the city.

The lightly armed Americans had yet to take the two hills. But Gage knew that they would certainly try to do so as soon as they had gathered enough ammunition and cannons for the job. He must beat them to the punch. He decided to make his move on June 17.

The general hoped that the river crossing would come as a surprise to the Americans. But it turned out to be nothing of the sort. Spies inside Boston learned of his intentions and passed the news to the Minutemen troops on the night of June 16. Led by Colonel William Prescott and gruff old General Israel Putnam, a veteran of the French and Indian War, about 2,000 of their number quickly left their camps, moved to the two hills, and spent the next hours furiously digging trenches and building breastworks (chest-high fortifications made of dirt, wood, and any other materials at hand). Their main line of defense took shape along the slopes of Breed's Hill. Bunker Hill would serve as a second defensive line in case they had to retreat.

When dawn broke, Gage was furious to see the American fortifications in the distance. His soldiers would have to fight to take the two hills.

Waiting for them behind the breastworks on Breed's Hill were 1,500 Americans. They sweated through a morn-

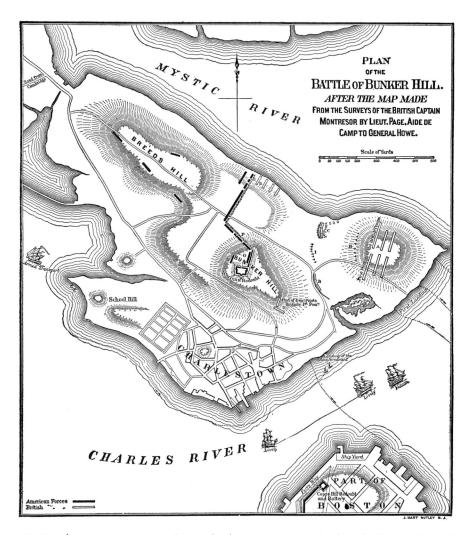

British surveys confused the names of the hills behind Charlestown. This map, based on those surveys, shows the names switched—the fortified hill just above the town is actually Breed's Hill, not Bunker Hill. But the battle fought there is still called the Battle of Bunker Hill.

British warships bombard Charlestown during the battle.

ing-long barrage from warships in the river and then, at noon, saw the British troops and artillery board long-boats and barges for the trip across to Charlestown. An hour later, the first of 2,500 redcoats, led by General William Howe, were landing near Charlestown. Artillerymen hauled their cannons ashore and took aim at the breast-works, but their guns remained silent. Somehow, the wrong ammunition had come across with the cannons.

General Howe sent his infantry and commanders fanning out along the shoreline and ordered them to attack the hill, with himself leading one of the units. Up at the breastworks, the men watched the redcoats climb toward them, scrambling over rail fences and threading their way among berry bushes as they came. The Britishers glanced at one another in surprise. They were expecting a hail of fire from the breastworks, but not a single musket ball was coming their way. The Americans had little ammunition and knew that they must make every shot count. They had been told not to fire until the last moment—until they saw the "whites" of the enemy's eyes.

Now, obeying the instructions, they waited patiently until the oncomers were just a few yards away. Suddenly, they heard the shouted order to fire. There was the crash of musketry and a rolling cloud of smoke all along the American line. Then came a second and a third crash as helpers handed them freshly loaded muskets (muskets fired one shot at a time and had to be reloaded before being fired again). For a long moment, the Americans were blinded by the smoke.

General Israel Putnam

As commander of the colonial troops at the Battle of Bunker Hill, Putnam is credited with one of the most famous military orders in American history. When he rode among his men just before the battle, he supposedly shouted: "Men, you are all marksmen; don't one of you fire until you see the whites of their eyes." No one can be certain that he actually gave that order.

They expected to see the British wave still washing toward them when the smoke cleared. Instead, they were greeted with the spectacle of bloodied enemy soldiers sprawled everywhere. Those still on their feet were fleeing back down the hill, jumping over bushes and fences as they went.

General Howe was horrified to see his troops in disarray. Throwing himself into their midst, he began restoring order, only to have their ranks splintered by sniper fire from Charlestown. Crews on the warships out in the river saw what was happening. Minutes later, hollow shells filled with pitch came raining in on Charlestown. The town burst into flames.

Once his troops were re-formed, Howe launched a second attack. Again, there was no American fire as the Britishers, panting in the afternoon heat, made their way up past the dead and wounded. Again, when they were within a few yards of the breastworks, there was the thunder of Minuteman muskets. And again, it sent the attackers reeling back down to the river.

Howe reassembled his troops once more, ordered a third attack, and led the way into that terrible silence. It continued all the way up to the rebel line. Then, instead of musket fire, there were yells as the Americans, now out of ammunition, met the oncomers with fists, rocks, and muskets swung like clubs. The fighting lasted but a few minutes before the outnumbered and out-gunned defenders turned and fled to Bunker Hill and then beyond.

The battle mistakenly went into the history books as the Battle of Bunker Hill. It was also mistakenly thought to be a British victory because the defenders had fled. In reality, it was a major American victory. It had cost Gage about 1,150 casualties, of whom 225 were killed. The American dead and wounded came to 450.

Abigail Adams

On the morning of June 17, 1775, Abigail Adams awoke to the sound of distant cannon fire. She roused her seven-year-old son and took him from their farm to a nearby spot where they could see the two hills that stood across the Charles River from Boston. They remained there the whole day and watched the battle of Breed's and Bunker hills. It was a sight the boy never forgot and that did much to shape his pride in his country. He was John Quincy Adams, who would one day become the nation's sixth president.

Abigail Adams has the distinction of being the only woman in American history who was the wife of one president and the mother of another. Her husband was the Revolutionary War statesman who was elected the nation's second president—John Adams. When Adams was a delegate to the Continental Congress, Abigail urged him to speak out against slavery, a practice she learned to detest during the Revolution. With America fighting for its freedom, she felt that slavery was contrary to the new nation's ideals.

[37]

A few days later, George Washington set out for Boston to take command of the Continental Army. It was a force that was to consist of small armies made up of colonial militia units and regular troops of volunteers; the regular troops were known as Continentals. The various armies would be assigned to areas throughout the colonies and would be commanded by generals answerable to Washington. Washington himself would lead one of the armies.

CHAPTER 4

1776

On reaching Boston in July 1775, Washington set up his headquarters at Cambridge, a village on the western bank of the Charles River. There were now some 20,000 Americans gathered around Boston, and he began to shape them into an army while he waited for the arrival of cannons that would enable him to lay siege to the city.

Those cannons had been seized some weeks earlier when a 200-man American force stormed and took distant Fort Ticonderoga, the British post that stood alongside Lake Champlain, which lies between New York and what is now Vermont. The cannons, however, were not to reach Washington for months. They were first used by two small armies that Congress sent to invade Canada.

The purpose of the strike was to grab Canada and deprive the British of a northern gateway through which to attack the rebelling colonies. It began successfully when one army, commanded by General Richard Montgomery, took the town of Montreal and moved on to Quebec. There, he met the second American force, which was led by Colonel Benedict Arnold.

Washington takes command of the Continental Army. Like many portrayals of the general, this one shows him as a hero.

Arnold's troops were exhausted and starving. They had struggled for endless miles through the thick woods in what would become the state of Maine, finally running so low on supplies that they had eaten their leather moccasins to stay alive. Nevertheless, Montgomery and Arnold launched an attack on Quebec on the last day of 1775. It proved to be a disaster. Montgomery was killed. Arnold sustained a wound in the leg. Their troops were cut to ribbons and the American threat to Canada came to an end.

And so, it was not until March 1776, that fifty pieces of artillery finally arrived at Cambridge after a back-breaking journey down from Canada through the snows of win-

Men and oxen struggle through the winter snow to bring artillery from Fort Ticonderoga to Boston.

ter. Washington immediately moved them to Dorchester Heights, which overlooked the heart of Boston, and then presented General William Howe, who had replaced Gage as the commander of the British forces, with a hard choice. The redcoats could leave the city or remain and be blasted to pieces. Howe stared up at the cannons. Then, to save not only his troops but the city as well, he placed his soldiers aboard warships and sailed off to Nova Scotia.

TOWARD A COMPLETE BREAK

In the months after Concord, the colonists suffered mixed feelings about the revolution. Many wanted a peaceful settlement of the problems with England, while many others were willing to take up arms for their rights as Britishers. Both groups were loyal to the mother country. But some colonists wanted a revolution that would lead to a complete break with Britain and the founding of America as an independent nation.

Those who wanted a complete break were few in number at the start of the fighting and were seen as hotheads by their fellow colonists. Their ranks, however, grew as 1775 turned into 1776. Three factors accounted for this growth.

First, on hearing of Concord and Breed's Hill, King George made a peaceful settlement impossible. Enraged, he declared the Americans to be in rebellion, a declaration that could end in the hanging of their leaders if ever they were captured.

Next, to give General Howe added muscle, he hired thousands of German soldiers (called Hessians) and sent them to America. The move shocked the colonials. They had always thought of the rebellion as a "family fight." But now George was pitting them against outsiders—outsiders with a nasty reputation for looting. (The Hessians, who were also known as mercenaries because they fought for another country for pay, proved to be good but brutal fighters; many grew so fond of America that they remained behind at war's end and became citizens.)

The third factor was a pamphlet titled *Common Sense*. Published in early 1776, it was written by fiery young Thomas Paine. In the slender booklet, he branded the colonists' mixed feelings as contrary to "common sense." Nowhere in the physical universe, he wrote, did smaller heavenly bodies control larger ones. Hence, there was no reason why tiny England should control the vast reaches of colonial America. Further, King George was the "Royal Brute of Britain." The colonies had the moral obligation to free themselves of this tyrant.

Thomas Paine's powerful writings fired the spirit of rebellion.

From the day of its publication, *Common Sense* proved to be a best-seller. More than 120,000 copies were purchased by June. That month, with more and more colonial sentiment now favoring a complete break with England, the Continental Congress took action.

JULY 4, 1776

The action began with one of Virginia's delegates—Richard Henry Lee. On June 7, he proposed that the Congress should adopt a resolution declaring the colonies to be "free and independent states." Lee's proposal triggered a debate among his fellow delegates that lasted almost a month. Some delegates favored the proposal; others still wanted to settle the problems with Britain without breaking away from the mother country. The proposal was finally adopted on July 2.

Technically, its adoption was all that was needed to break the ties with England. But, on first hearing the proposal in June, the delegates had decided that, if it were adopted, it should be accompanied by a written "Declaration of Independence." They assigned a committee of five members to prepare the document.

The task of writing the declaration went to a tall, sandy-haired Virginia lawyer who was known for his writing skills—Thomas Jefferson. The words that flowed from his pen were reviewed and amended by fellow committee members Benjamin Franklin of Pennsylvania and John Adams of Massachusetts. Then his work went before the Congress for discussion.

What the Congress received was a document that began by speaking of human rights. It went on to say that

The committee that drew up the Declaration of Independence was made up of (from left): Thomas Jefferson of Virginia, Roger Sherman of Connecticut, Benjamin Franklin of Pennsylvania, Robert Livingston of New York, and John Adams of Massachusetts. Jefferson did most of the writing.

King George had violated these rights and that, as a consequence, the Americans colonies were justified in separating from the mother country. Then came a list of those violations. They included unjust taxation, the establishment of a military dictatorship in the colonies, and the curtailing of colonial trade.

[45]

Thomas Jefferson

It was to Jefferson that the principal task of writing the Declaration of Independence fell. He served as the governor of Virginia during the war. He later became the nation's first secretary of state and its third president. His final years were devoted to founding the University of Virginia. He designed its buildings and supervised its construction.

The document ended with the ringing statement that Congress, on behalf of the American people, was now declaring:

> . . . that these United Colonies are, and of right ought to be, *Free and Independent States*; that they are absolved from all allegiance to the British crown, and that all political connection between them and the state of Great Britain is, and ought to be, totally dissolved . . .

The Declaration was approved and signed by the fifty-six delegates to the Congress. With the signing, the thirteen British colonies ceased to exist. A new nation, the United States of America, was born.

But not all colonists liked that new nation. Thousands remained faithful to the Crown. Known as Tories or Loyalists, they would be roughly treated by the Americans throughout the revolution, with some 80,000 of their number being driven off to Canada. About 50,000 others would fight alongside the redcoats, serve as spies for them, or incite the Indians to harass the Americans.

They would add much to the trouble that the infant country was to suffer in the coming years of warfare.

CHAPTER 5

The Road to Trenton

From mid-1776 to late 1778, the war was fought mainly in the northern and middle states, from the lands adjoining Canada down to Pennsylvania. They were years that featured two major campaigns ordered by the British government in London.

The first called for a two-pronged invasion from Canada. General Guy Carleton was to follow the river passage from Quebec south to Lake Champlain and then sweep on through the Hudson River Valley. At the same time, General Howe was to sail down the Atlantic from Nova Scotia, capture New York City, and then march north and meet Carleton. The whole idea was to split Massachusetts off from the states to the south. Surely, the British government thought, once divided the states would give up the war.

CARLETON ON LAKE CHAMPLAIN

With 9,000 troops sailing aboard small warships, Carleton moved along the St. Lawrence River and turned into the

Richelieu River, which flowed into Lake Champlain. But while coasting down the 100-mile- (160-kilometer-) long lake on October 11, he ran into a small fleet of American boats commanded by Benedict Arnold.

They presented a sorry sight. They were small, rickety, and top heavy with the cannons lashed to their decks. Under Arnold's supervision, they had been built of felled trees by woodsmen and soldiers while awaiting Carleton's arrival. Now they came out to fight when Carleton appeared at noon. The two fleets opened fire with their cannons, with both sides taking direct hits. A cloud of blinding smoke rolled over the boats. They groped through the blackish muck all afternoon, firing at anything they sighted and coming so close together that they began trading musket shots.

By nightfall, Arnold's "homemade" fleet had been torn apart by the superior British guns. Under the cover of

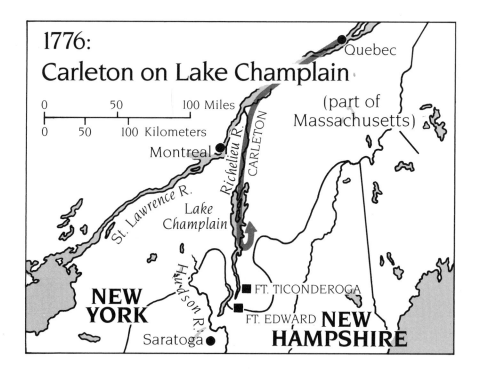

1776:
Carleton on Lake Champlain

darkness, he tried to escape south with his few remaining boats to his base at Fort Ticonderoga. But Carleton gave chase and destroyed them one by one.

Arnold finally led a few survivors to Ticonderoga. His British pursuer, however, stopped short of the fort. Carleton knew that the snows of winter were fast approaching and would make campaigning impossible. He turned back to Canada, planning to return the following spring.

HOWE AT NEW YORK

General Howe sailed from Nova Scotia in the summer of 1776. He reached his destination in late June and anchored off the southern tip of Long Island, which lay just across the East River from Manhattan Island.

Waiting for him on Long Island was George Washington. Knowing New York to be an important port that would surely be a major British target, Washington had

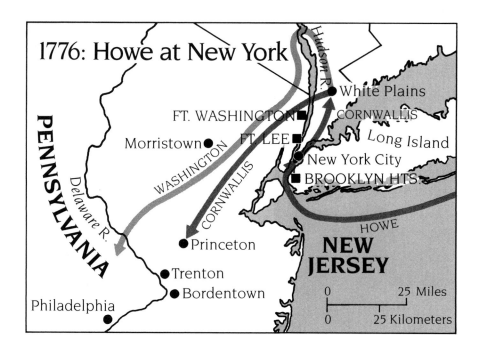

brought an army of 18,000 men there weeks before. He had stationed them at points throughout Manhattan Island. On Long Island itself, they were entrenched on Brooklyn Heights, a summit that overlooked New York.

Though Howe arrived in June, he did not attack for several weeks. He was commanding 32,000 men who had to be carried aboard 400 transports and 73 warships from both Nova Scotia and Britain. It was not until August that they were all in place and he gave the order to storm Brooklyn Heights. When the attack came, the Americans fought back savagely but were forced to retreat. Howe might well have destroyed Washington's army right then had he pressed on and cornered the fleeing troops. But he decided to stop and rest his redcoats for a day or so before striking again.

The delay gave Washington the chance to escape. He gathered his troops together and, under the cover of fog and darkness, ferried them over to New York. Howe soon came after him, took the city, and drove the Americans into another retreat. Fighting a rear-guard action all the way, Washington slowly moved north to two small forts that he had earlier built alongside the Hudson River: Fort Washington on Manhattan Island itself and Fort Lee on the opposite shore.

Stationing some of his men at each fort, the general left Manhattan Island and headed north into the mainland of New York state. He had learned that Howe had bypassed him by sailing up the East River to the mainland. The Britisher was now marching west to cut off any escape route from the two forts. Washington's plan was to intercept him and turn him back.

The plan failed. When the two commanders met and fought at White Plains in late October, the victory went

American forces retreat at the Battle of Long Island in August, 1776.

to Howe. Washington was forced to retreat farther north. Howe turned his attention to Forts Washington and Lee. After bitter fighting, both fell into British hands.

THE CHASE

Now pursuing Washington as he fled north was one of Howe's ablest generals, Charles Cornwallis. The Virginian went as far as Peekskill and then decided that his best course lay in swinging about and trying to find safety from Cornwallis's superior numbers by crossing the Delaware River into Pennsylvania.

He moved to the west side of the Hudson River and turned southwest, gave New York City a wide berth, and headed down through New Jersey. Throughout November, Cornwallis snapped at his heels. To delay the Britisher's wagons and artillery, the Americans burned every bridge they crossed and sent one tree after another toppling across the roadway with their axes. They worked furiously, knowing that the British front ranks were often less than a mile behind them.

At last, in early December, they came to the Delaware River, which separated New Jersey and Pennsylvania. Roaming for miles along its banks, they grabbed every boat they would require for the westward crossing over into Pennsylvania. Left behind in flames was every vessel not needed for the trip.

By the time Cornwallis reached the Delaware, Washington had found the safety he had sought. He was camped on the Pennsylvania side, with the "boatless" British general stranded over on the New Jersey banks. This did not worry Cornwallis, however. He spread his redcoats out for several miles along the river. Then he left them in the snows of winter, went to New York City, and prepared to sail home to England. General Cornwallis felt certain that the Americans were beaten and that the fighting was almost over.

Events soon proved him wrong.

VICTORY AT TRENTON

Washington now took stock of his situation, and he did not like what he saw. His troops were battered and exhausted, their clothes in rags and their shoes in tatters, from the long march. After all the defeats suffered since Long Island, many thought that their cause was lost. They had little heart for more fighting. The army was made up of militia units and volunteers, and Washington was deeply worried about the volunteers. They had signed up for short periods of duty and now their enlistments were about to expire. They were sure to leave him when the time came.

The Virginian knew that he must do something to instill a fresh fighting spirit in the men. He had to stagger the British with an attack that would end in an American victory. But where could he strike?

Washington got his answer when he learned that 3,000 Hessians were stationed in the little town of Trenton just across the river. He decided to hit them with a three-pronged attack on the morning of December 26. During the night, he would ferry 2,500 men over to the far bank at a point 6 miles (nearly 10 kilometers) north of Trenton. Another group would cross directly to the town itself. A third would land to the south. Then they would strike at dawn.

The date of the attack was a wise choice. The Hessians were sure to be off their guard, sleeping off the effects of celebrating Christmas. But Christmas night turned out to be a disastrous one. Wind-driven snow and sleet lashed the men as they manhandled their cannons aboard the 30-foot (9-meter) boats for the river trip and climbed aboard themselves. Then, once free of the shore, they had to fight off the ice floes that came sweeping in on the boats, threatening to capsize them. So difficult was the crossing that only Washington's group landed on the New Jersey side. The other two were stopped by the floes and the rough water.

On landing, Washington had only his 2,500 men. But he thrust aside any thoughts of abandoning the attack.

CONTINENTAL MARCH
Sons of 1776.

composed by

JAMES E. MAGRUDER

PUBLISHED BY **MILLER & BEACHAM** BALTIMORE

Lith. by A. Hoen & Co Balt?

Entered according to act of Congress A.D 1861 by Miller & Beacham in the Clerks office of the District Court of Md.

George Washington's crossing of the Delaware is one of the most fabled events in American history. Here, a copy of Emanuel Leutze's famous painting of the scene is reproduced on a sheet music cover from the 1860s.

He quickly divided his small force into two units. He sent one moving stealthily past the town to strike from the south, and the second group on a different route for a strike from the north.

The 6-mile (almost 10-kilometer) hike to Trenton began. The men cursed as the ice on the roadway cut into what was left of their shoes or the strips of blankets that those without shoes had wrapped around their feet. Their muskets became soaked with snow and promised not to fire when needed. Washington ordered the men to fight with their bayonets.

By dawn, both groups were in their assigned positions and launched the attack. Both stumbled upon the few sentries who were guarding the outskirts of Trenton and charged into them with their bayonets. There was shouting as the sentries were driven from their posts. A Hessian officer raced into town to warn his commanding officer, Colonel Johann Rall, of what was happening. Though roused from a deep sleep after a night of celebrating, Rall quickly dressed and rushed outside to collect his men for a counterattack. Everywhere, he saw confusion as the soldiers, still groggy with sleep, stumbled into the streets and struggled into their uniforms.

As Rall was desperately assembling his men, the Americans plunged into Trenton. Rumbling behind them came four cannons that were quickly placed at the heads of two main streets—two guns to a street. Rall sighted the field pieces on one street and yelled for his men to seize them. The soldiers obeyed, only to be cut down by grapeshot when the cannons erupted. Then the American gunners saw a German cannon swing into position at the opposite end of the street. Before it could fire, two young officers—Captain William Washington and Lieutenant James Monroe (later to be President Monroe)—sprinted forward with a handful of soldiers and sent its crew fleeing.

Meanwhile, some Americans took refuge in houses. Rubbing their muskets dry, they began sniping at the Hessians outside.

Washington leads the troops in this idealized version of the action at Trenton.

Two musket balls struck Colonel Rall. He fell to the ground fatally wounded.

Charging with bayonets, and assisted by the sniper fire from the houses, the Americans pressed into the center of Trenton. The Hessians, still shaken by the sudden attack, realized that it would be impossible to repel the Americans. One by one, they began to surrender. In the next minutes, the fighting ended. It had lasted less than an hour.

Washington was jubilant. Not one of his men had died in the battle and only four had been injured. But 90 Hessians had been wounded and 25 killed. Into American hands had fallen about 950 prisoners, plus Trenton's valuable military stores. The general knew that he had given his bedraggled troops exactly the victory they needed.

A NEW VICTORY

Washington's jubilation was short-lived, however. A few days after bringing the rest of his army over to Trenton, he learned that Cornwallis, on hearing what had happened, had canceled his trip to England and hurried to rejoin his troops. With more than 5,000 men, he was now marching on Trenton.

Cornwallis arrived on January 2, 1777, and positioned his troops for an assault the following day. Washington elected not to defend Trenton but to attempt a daring offensive of his own. It would take him behind the enemy lines for an attack on the town of Princeton some 10 miles (16 kilometers) to the northeast. Cornwallis's march had started from there, and Washington was certain that the Britisher had left just a few men behind to defend the town.

On the night of January 2, Washington succeeded in a neat bit of trickery. Leaving his campfires burning brightly to fool the British into thinking that his men were bedding down for the night, he led a dead-silent march around Cornwallis's flank and struck at Princeton the next morning. He was right in thinking that the town was lightly defended. Only 700 redcoats were there and the

This German engraving shows Hessian troops that were captured by American forces at the Battle of Trenton.

Americans quickly put them to flight. Washington then collected many of the supplies that they left behind and marched northwest to Morristown, where his weary troops settled down for the rest of the winter. They were joined by troops that had remained in the New York colony.

Much of 1776 had gone badly for Washington, but it had ended on a triumphant note. As a result, many of his volunteers reenlisted and many new volunteers poured into Morristown to join him in the fighting that the new year would bring.

A New Campaign

In early 1777, the British government devised a new campaign against the Americans. The idea behind it was the same as the failed 1776 plan: to drive a wedge between the states. This time, however, the aim was not to isolate Massachusetts. Instead, invading forces from Canada were to take control of New York State.

Three armies were to make up the invasion force. The first would be led by General John Burgoyne. Following Carleton's 1776 route, he was to drive the rebels from Lake Champlain, and continue south. The second, commanded by General Howe, was to thrust up the Hudson River from New York City. The third, led by Lieutenant Colonel Barry St. Leger, was to strike out from Canada west of Burgoyne, capture the town of Oswego, and then move eastward. The three forces were to meet at the city of Albany.

From there, the British could bring all of New York under their thumb and cut New York off from the rest of the states.

BURGOYNE'S CAMPAIGN

With 7,200 Britishers and Hessians, Burgoyne launched his campaign in June and moved down Lake Champlain to Fort Ticonderoga. In command of the 2,500 Americans there was General Arthur St. Clair, who realized that he did not have enough men to repel the redcoated army that swung into view. After a brief exchange of musket fire, he retreated to Fort Edward, 20 miles (32 kilometers) to his south. Ticonderoga fell to Burgoyne on July 5.

Burgoyne set out confidently for Fort Edward, but now he ran into trouble. Philip Schuyler, the American general in command of the region, sent 1,000 men with axes to do to Burgoyne what Washington had done to Cornwallis the year before: delay his advance. They felled trees across his path. They dammed streams and flooded the lowlands around him. Burgoyne's infantry was slowed to a crawl. Worse, his supply wagons were slowed even more. They dropped far behind the marchers. Soon, the infantrymen began to run out of food.

The food situation became so desperate that Burgoyne dispatched 1,000 men southeast to Bennington (in present-day Vermont) to pillage the town for supplies. Instead of finding what they needed, they encountered an American unit commanded by General John Stark. The redcoats suffered such a thrashing at his hands that only 100 of their number stumbled back to Burgoyne. They arrived empty-handed.

When the English general reached Fort Edward, Schuyler left the post to him and withdrew south to the point near the town of Saratoga. Burgoyne, angry over the Bennington defeat, set out after his enemy, overtook him in September, and found him strongly entrenched. Never-

Burgoyne surrenders to Gates. The British general was known to his troops and the Americans as "Gentleman Johnny" because of his courtly manners and expensive tastes. He spent his last years writing and was a recognized playwright.

theless, Burgoyne attacked immediately, only to be repulsed. In a series of battles and skirmishes during the next days, he sustained such heavy losses that he withdrew for a distance, settled down, and sent a message south for General Howe to bring reinforcements. For a reason we'll see later, Howe never came to his aid. In October, with his troops facing starvation and under attack on all sides, Burgoyne surrendered to General Horatio Gates, who had just replaced Schuyler and now took credit for the victory that Schuyler had actually won.

ST. LEGER'S CAMPAIGN

St. Leger's contingent of 2,500 men was the smallest of the three British armies. Like Burgoyne, he moved out of Canada in June. After sailing down the St. Lawrence River and along the shoreline of Lake Ontario, he reached his first objective, Oswego, in July. There, a large force of Tories (colonists who were faithful to the Crown) and Iroquois Indians joined him. With them, he marched eastward to Fort Stanwix, the American installation that loomed in his path to Albany. He expected the Stanwix troops to surrender when they saw how greatly they were outnumbered. He was due for a disappointment.

On reaching the fort in early August, St. Leger found that the six hundred American defenders had no thought of surrendering. They were well fortified and ready for a long siege—a siege that was to last for weeks. A few days after his arrival, St. Leger received ominous news. He was told that a nearby militia leader, the aged Nicholas Herkimer, was marching to the rescue of Stanwix with eight hundred men. Immediately, the Britisher sent his Tories and Indians to meet the old general and drive him off.

That meeting took place at Oriskany, a few miles southeast of Stanwix. What resulted was one of the bloodiest battles of the war.

The Tories and Iroquois concealed themselves in the woods that lay to either side of the road to Stanwix. When Herkimer's mile-long column passed between them, they trapped it in a sudden and deadly crossfire. Shocked and confused, some of the Americans retreated, but soon regrouped and returned. The survivors of that first musket blast charged into the woods and fought hand-to-hand with the attackers. Knives, bayonets, rifle

[64]

butts, and tomahawks—all played a terrible role in what turned out to be a six-hour battle. At one point, Herkimer fell with a bullet in his leg. He crawled to a nearby tree, propped himself up, and, with his pipe clamped between his teeth, went on directing his men.

Hearing the sounds of battle in the distance, the Americans at Stanwix triggered an action of their own. They burst out of the fort and attacked St. Leger's camp, striking hard and putting the redcoats to flight. Then they gathered as many supplies as possible, and escaped back

Mortally wounded, Herkimer directs the fighting at Oriskany.

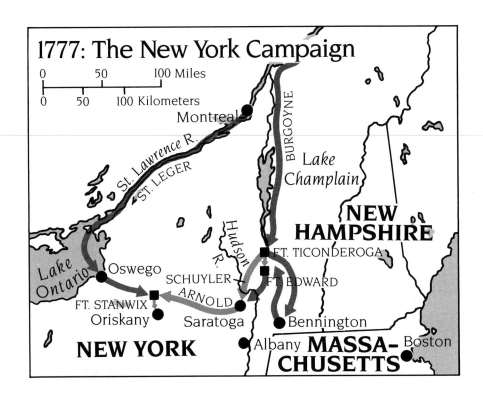

1777: The New York Campaign

0 50 100 Miles

0 50 100 Kilometers

Montreal

St. Lawrence R.

ST. LEGER

BURGOYNE

Lake Champlain

NEW HAMPSHIRE

Lake Ontario

Oswego

Hudson R.

SCHUYLER

ARNOLD

FT. TICONDEROGA

FT. EDWARD

FT. STANWIX

Oriskany

Saratoga

Bennington

Albany

NEW YORK

MASSA-CHUSETTS

Boston

to safety before St. Leger could rally his men and retake the camp. The Americans now had additional food and arms for the siege.

Over at Oriskany, the Iroquois quit the fighting at nightfall and faded into the woods. Left alone, the Tories broke away and hurried back to Stanwix. The battle had gone to the Americans, but they had lost a third of their number and had to return to their home base. General Herkimer died of his wound ten days later. The siege continued.

Near Saratoga far to the east, General Schuyler heard the news of what was happening at Stanwix. He called for volunteers to march to the relief of the post. Benedict Arnold, now a major general, quickly asked for and received permission to lead the rescue force. He was always ready for action and wanted to make up for his defeats at Quebec in 1775 and on Lake Champlain in 1776.

With some 900 men, Arnold raced toward Stanwix in mid-August. As he marched, he devised a plan that might rout St. Leger without a fight. On capturing a young slow-witted Dutchman, he made the boy promise to go to the British camp and spread word that a huge American army was bearing down on Stanwix. The youngster's brother was to be held hostage and would be killed if the messenger failed to do as instructed.

The plan was a cruel and brilliant one—and it worked. When the boy burst into the camp and screamed word of the approaching army, the Britishers asked how many soldiers were coming. Staring wildly at the surrounding woods, he replied, "As many as there are leaves on the trees." Panic spread everywhere. The Iroquois fled, with many of the Tories racing after them. The news so rattled St. Leger that he withdrew his troops on August 22 and returned to Canada.

Sybil Ludington

Sybil Ludington was born and raised in Putnam County, New York, where her father commanded a local military unit. In April 1777, a messenger arrived at her family home with the news that a British force was advancing on nearby Danbury, Connecticut, and planning to capture the military stores that her father's regiment kept there. Because the messenger was exhausted and could travel no farther, Sybil mounted her horse and galloped through the night, calling her father's troops to arms. The men hurried to Danbury but were too late to stop the British from looting and burning the town. Later, however, they participated in a battle in which the British suffered 200 casualties.

Sybil's journey surpassed Paul Revere's famous ride on the night of April 18, 1775. It covered more than 40 miles (64 kilometers)—outdistancing Revere's trip by an estimated 15 miles (24 kilometers).

HOWE'S CAMPAIGN

Howe did not send reinforcements to Burgoyne at Saratoga for a simple reason. He was not marching up the Hudson River that September and never received Burgoyne's call for help. Rather, he was moving into Pennsylvania.

The British general had decided to take Philadelphia before venturing up the Hudson to meet with Burgoyne and St. Leger. He felt that the capture of the rebel capital would demoralize the Americans and that his campaign to take the city would also help Burgoyne. It would prevent Washington from moving his army to the Saratoga battlefront.

Howe began his move against Philadelphia in June. He attempted to march across New Jersey but was so harassed by Washington that he returned to New York City in disgust. He then decided to head for Philadelphia by sea. He would sail down the Atlantic, swing into Delaware Bay, coast up to the entrance of the Delaware River, and then proceed along the river to Philadelphia.

General William Howe

After leading the three assaults on Breed's Hill, Howe replaced General Gage as the commander of the British forces in America. His attack on New York City came from the sea, with ships arriving from Boston and England. At that time, his force was the biggest ever sent overseas by Britain. Howe served in Parliament prior to the Revolution and opposed Britain's oppressive measures against the colonies. During the war, it was rumored that he was secretly sympathetic to the Americans.

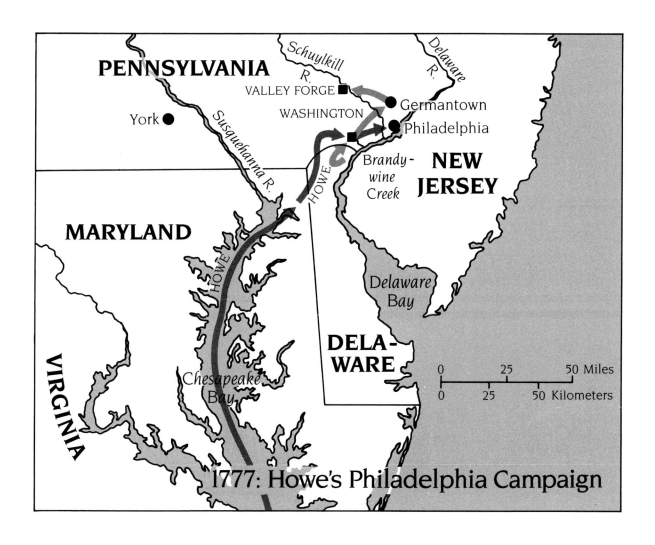

1777: Howe's Philadelphia Campaign

With 15,000 British and Hessian troops aboard 260 ships, Howe put to sea on July 23. But adverse winds scattered the fleet and he did not reach Delaware Bay until early August, at which time he changed plans. He heard the Americans had fortified the Delaware River and that passage along it to the rebel capital would be suicide for his ships. Instead, he took his fleet to Chesapeake Bay, sailed to its northern end, and put his men ashore in mid-August. Ahead of them lay a 50-mile (80-kilometer) march to their objective. In Philadelphia, Congress began moving to York, Pennsylvania.

Once Howe was sighted on Chesapeake Bay, Washington knew that his foe planned an overland march on Philadelphia and quickly moved to intercept him. He settled his men—nearly 12,000 in all—on Brandywine Creek, a tributary of the Delaware River, and waited for the enemy marchers to arrive. When Howe finally appeared on September 11, he confused the Americans by sending a Hessian force on a noisy maneuver in front of them. While they were watching, the main body of his troops stole around the rebel flank and struck from the rear. The Americans, outmanuevered and outnumbered, broke into a retreat to the north.

Howe marched on to Philadelphia, fighting skirmishes as he went, and took possession of the city on September 26. Once settled in his new headquarters, he sent a large force of redcoats and Hessians to destroy the fortifications that the Americans had built along the Delaware River. He realized that the job of hauling supplies overland to his troops from Chesapeake Bay would be a backbreaking·and time-consuming one. It would be far easier to sail them up the Delaware. He must have the river.

Washington, stinging at the defeat he had suffered at Brandywine, now wanted to balance the score with a victory of his own. For the scene of that victory, he selected Germantown, a village located about 5 miles (8 kilometers) north of Philadelphia. Howe had stationed a large segment of his army there.

Washington divided his troops into four units and attacked before dawn on a foggy October 4. At first, striking with surprise, his men drove the British out of the village. Victory seemed within his grasp. But a tragic mistake snatched it away. Two of his forces, groping blindly through the fog and smoke of battle, stumbled into each other, each mistaking the other for the enemy. They ex-

Betsy Ross

Legend surrounds Elizabeth (Betsy) Ross, a Pennsylvania seamstress and upholsterer. She has gone down in history as the woman who, at the request of George Washington, sewed the first American flag. Perhaps Washington did ask her to make the flag. Perhaps not. No one really knows. All that can be said is that she did fashion several flags for the general's army.

changed fire and gave the British time to regroup and counterattack. Confused by the tragic error, Washington's men were unable to defend themselves. They retreated. Soon thereafter, he led them to Valley Forge, some 20 miles (32 kilometers) northwest of Philadelphia, and settled them into camp for the winter.

In the meantime, the force that Howe had sent to the Delaware River attacked the major American stronghold there, Fort Mercer. The Americans fought back for several weeks, taking a heavy toll in British and Hessian lives before being forced to retreat and leave the installation in enemy hands. At the same time, the British force struck at the American ships and traps (made of nets and logs) in the river and at the nearby camps and fortifications. In November, Howe called off the fighting for the year. His troops were comfortably quartered in Philadelphia and he controlled the Delaware River from the rebel capital down to Delaware Bay.

From Valley Forge to Virginia

The winter was a terrible one for the 10,000 troops at Valley Forge. They shivered in makeshift huts and huddled around small campfires. Many tried to stay awake all night for fear of freezing to death if they fell asleep. They had little to eat and once went without even bread for three successive days. Their clothes and footwear were in ruins. Some 2,500 of the men had no shoes whatsoever and kept their feet bound in blanket strips. By the spring of 1778, one of every four men at Valley Forge had died.

Why were they made to suffer so? There were several reasons. When food was collected at distant marketplaces, there were often no wagons to haul it to Valley Forge. Manufactured clothing and shoes were scarce in a country where the people lived mainly by farming. Congress had precious little money to spend on the Continentals. And the states, which were supposed to provision their militia units, were also short of money.

Worst of all, many American merchants and manufacturers put the desire for profit above loyalty to their country. They sold their wares to the British, who could

Baron von Steuben drills the troops at Valley Forge.

pay in gold while all that Congress could offer was the almost worthless paper money that it printed. When the troops were freezing at Valley Forge, some Bostonians made profits of up to 200 percent by selling army clothing to the British.

But the winter also had a positive side to it. At Valley Forge were several foreign officers who had come to America's aid, among them Germany's Baron Friedrich von Steuben and France's Marquis de Lafayette. They were all experienced military men and they spent the winter sharpening the fighting skills of the Americans. Especially popular was the portly von Steuben, who drilled the men endlessly. The Americans, while good fighters, had always suffered from a lack of military training. When Washington's army emerged from Valley Forge, it was—thanks largely to von Steuben—a better fighting force than ever before.

A SUDDEN CHANGE

Though the Americans were improved fighters by the dawn of 1778, their morale was frighteningly low after the icy weeks of starvation. But then came a sudden change that lifted their spirits. In February, the French king, Louis XVI, signed treaties in which he recognized America as an independent nation and agreed to support it in the war. The pact led to France providing America with troops, a fleet of warships, and more than $2 million in aid.

Actually, France had been secretly supplying powder and arms to the rebels since 1776. But now Louis came out in open support of the Americans. He did so because the victory at Saratoga convinced him and his ministers that the rebels might indeed win the war against France's long-time enemy. Louis and his ministers knew that French help could keep the rebels fighting.

He also knew that the British had been stunned by Saratoga. They, too, now thought that the upstart rebels might miraculously win the war. Consequently, Parliament had just passed an important act that tried to do two things at the same time: avoid a humiliating defeat and bring the colonies back to the mother country. It granted to the Americans all the freedoms they wanted—except complete independence. In the end, the measure came to nothing. It was too late to stop the Americans from wanting to have a nation of their own.

[75]

The Marquis de Lafayette and Baron Friedrich von Steuben

Lafayette (above) and von Steuben (right) were with Washington at Valley Forge and in the fierce fighting that led to the decisive victory at Yorktown.

Lafayette's forces played a key role in that victory.

Because von Steuben vigorously drilled the men at Valley Forge into better soldiers than they had ever been before, he became affectionately known as "the father of the United States Army."

Greatly responsible for the French decision to back the revolution was seventy-two-year-old Benjamin Franklin. In 1776, Congress had sent him to France as a representative of America. There, his wit and charm had paved the way to the treaties.

Benjamin Franklin is received at the French court in 1778.

King Louis's decision had an immediate effect on the redcoats in Philadelphia. The British government feared France would soon send a fleet to blockade Delaware Bay and seal it off from the ships that were bringing supplies to the city. General Henry Clinton, who had replaced Howe as the British military commander in America, was ordered to abandon the city and return to New York City.

Clinton obeyed and left in June. Washington pursued him across New Jersey, met him in battle at Monmouth on a blistering hot June 28. After fighting Clinton to a draw, he followed him the rest of the way to his destination. Establishing his headquarters at White Plains, Washington placed his troops around New York City to watch his adversary and keep him hemmed in. It was the start of a vigil that was to last for three years—until 1781.

DISTANT FIGHTING

While Washington watched, there was fighting at points distant from his headquarters.

Out on the western frontier, the settlers were being terrorized by Indian tribes allied with the British. Starting in June 1778, George Rogers Clark, a young Kentucky patriot, tried to end the problem by leading a small band in the successful capture of three enemy posts—Forts Kaskaskia, Cahokia, and Vincennes—in what are now the states of Illinois and Indiana. Equally important, he captured Colonel Henry Hamilton, the British governor of the region. Ever since the war's beginning, Hamilton had promoted the Indian attacks by offering bounties for any Americans killed. Clark's work did not end the Indian problem but did weaken the British hold on the frontier.

Molly Pitcher

Molly Pitcher was the nickname given to Mary McCauley. She followed her husband to the war and won the nickname for her practice of bringing water to the thirsty troops while they were on the march or in battle. She is also said to have replaced her husband at his cannon when he fell wounded during the 1778 battle at Monmouth, New Jersey. It is not known whether the story of her feat is true or legend.

Both 1778 and 1779 brought victories for the infant American navy, which had been established soon after the formation of the Continental Army. For most of the war, the navy consisted of small ships, such as those built on Lake Champlain by Benedict Arnold and those that had blockaded the Delaware River against Howe's advance on Philadelphia. Beginning in 1778, however, a young sea captain, John Paul Jones, brought the war to Britain itself when he raided English and Scottish seaports. Then, in 1779, with four ships in his fleet, he met a large enemy force off Britain's northeast coast and captured the fifty-gun frigate *Serapis* after a three-hour battle at point-blank range.

The *Bonhomme Richard* and the *Serapis* locked in battle.

John Paul Jones

Jones was serving as captain of the *Bonhomme Richard*, an old French ship that had been given to the Americans, when he captured the fifty-five-gun British frigate *Serapis*. His victory was the young U.S. Navy's greatest in the war. Catherine the Great later appointed him a rear admiral in the Russian navy.

Though his victories were proud ones, Jones actually did little damage to the British. Far greater harm was done by the thousand privately owned ships that augmented the navy's strength. With Congressional permission, they prowled the Atlantic, attacking and plundering enemy merchant shipping. In all, they captured some 600 British prizes.

Late 1780, however, brought Washington news that stunned him. He learned that one of his most daring fighters, Benedict Arnold, had defected to the British. Always an ambitious man, Arnold had been angered by the suspicion that his military talents were being ignored and that he was being passed over for promotion. Further, deep in debt, he desperately needed money. Consequently, he plotted to turn West Point, the stronghold that he commanded on the Hudson River, over to the British for a cash payment. The plot was accidentally discovered and Arnold fled to the British ranks.

A NEW BRITISH PLAN

We must now turn back to 1778 to see the start of the campaign that eventually led to America's final victory in the war. That year, the British government came up with a new plan of conquest. Having failed to split the states by subduing Massachusetts and New York, the government decided to concentrate on the southern states, which were thought to be the home of thousands of Tories. The hope was that the Tories would join the redcoats in sweeping northward from Georgia to overwhelm Washington's forces and bring the war to an end.

Benedict Arnold

Arnold was given the assignment of building the small American fleet that defended Lake Champlain against General Guy Carleton because he had made several merchant voyages as a young man. Distinguishing himself in a number of battles, he became one of Washington's most prized officers, only to shock and dishearten the commander by turning traitor and siding with the British.

Patriot Wives

During the Revolution, Martha Washington (above) lived at her husband's headquarters at Cambridge, Massachusetts. But she always joined him when he went into winter quarters at the end of each year and remained with him until the fighting began again in the spring. She did much to cheer the soldiers throughout the icy months, knitting socks for them and mending their tattered clothes. During the terrible stay at Valley Forge, while occupying a nearby stone house with Washington, she was seen daily walking among the sick and wounded, handing them bits of food from the basket she always carried and stopping to talk with each for a few minutes.

Several other wives joined their husbands during that hard winter of 1777–78. One was Lucy Knox, who was married to Henry Knox, Washington's commander of artillery in several campaigns. Another was Kitty Greene, the wife of one of Washington's most talented generals, Nathanael Greene, who fought so successfully against Cornwallis in the southern campaign that brought the Revolution to a close.

The sprightly Lucy Knox was the subject of a story that might be legend. Soon after the war broke out, she and her husband were riding in a carriage that had to pass through a British roadblock. Knowing that the carriage was sure to be searched, Lucy is said to have sewn Henry's sword into her petticoats before leaving home so that the redcoats would not find it and detain them as suspected rebels.

Actually, the British had attempted to gain a toehold in the southern states two years earlier, in 1776, by sending an invasion fleet against Charleston, South Carolina. When the invaders were repulsed, Britain had turned its attention to the Massachusetts and New York campaigns. Now, the south was to take center stage again.

The 1778 campaign began in December, when General Clinton sent a force of 3,500 men sailing down from New York City to sweep ashore near Savannah, Georgia. The American troops in the town were commanded by General Robert Howe (no relation to Britain's General Howe) and were outnumbered four to one by the invaders. Nevertheless, Howe had them take up positions on the road leading up from the shore. Howe thought it a fine spot for a defensive action because swampland that the British were sure to find impenetrable lay to each side. But one redcoated unit managed to locate a path through the swamp and struck him from the rear while the main enemy force attacked head-on. The town fell by nightfall on December 29.

The invaders immediately thrust inland and took Augusta in January 1779. Then, in the next months, the fighting spread throughout Georgia. It was vicious fighting that saw Tories flock to the aid of the British while patriot backwoodsmen and farmers joined the Americans. Relatives and neighbors fought each other, often to the death. In September, an American force under General Benjamin Lincoln attempted to retake Savannah but was driven off.

In February 1780, General Clinton sailed from New York with General Cornwallis and 8,700 redcoats and Hessians, landed at South Carolina, attacked Charleston, and took the city in May. Clinton then returned to New York

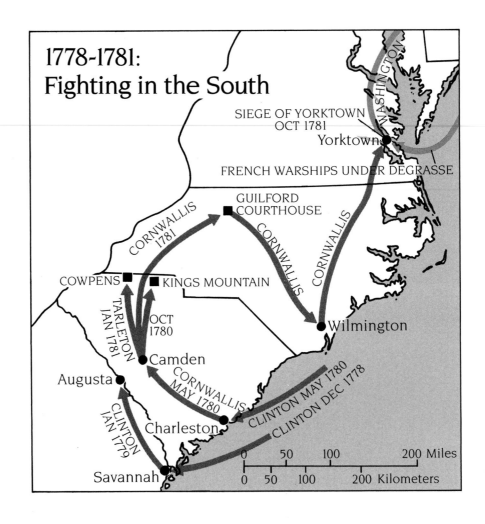

1778-1781: Fighting in the South

SIEGE OF YORKTOWN
OCT 1781

WASHINGTON

Yorktown

FRENCH WARSHIPS UNDER DEGRASSE

GUILFORD
COURTHOUSE

CORNWALLIS
1781

CORNWALLIS

CORNWALLIS

COWPENS ■ KINGS MOUNTAIN

TARLETON
JAN 1781

OCT
1780

Wilmington

Camden

Augusta

CORNWALLIS
MAY 1780

CLINTON MAY 1780

CLINTON DEC 1778

CLINTON
JAN 1779

Charleston

| 0 | 50 | 100 | 200 Miles |

| 0 | 50 | 100 | 200 Kilometers |

Savannah

City and left the job of conquering the south to Cornwallis.

Cornwallis immediately set out for Camden, some 100 miles (160 kilometers) northwest of Charleston. On reaching the town, an advance unit took it over and settled down to await their commander's arrival with the main force. In the meantime, General Horatio Gates, who had accepted Burgoyne's surrender at Saratoga and was now commanding the army in the south, heard of what was happening at Camden and hurried there to recapture it before Cornwallis arrived. But when he ran into the British general one night and attacked, he so mishandled his troops that he was soundly thrashed and forced to flee.

After resting his men for a time, Cornwallis moved toward his next target, North Carolina. Everywhere, in the midst of what was thought to be Tory country, he met stiff resistance from patriot groups. Small bands of Americans, led by such men as Francis Marion and Thomas Sumter, did everything possible to hamper his progress. Fighting a guerrilla war, they sniped at his redcoats and Hessians from the surrounding trees and rocks. They attacked his supply wagons. They struck at his outposts and scouting parties.

Though they slowed Cornwallis's progress, the Americans did not have the manpower to stop him completely. By September, he was approaching the North Carolina border. He now put Major Patrick Ferguson in charge of 1,100 redcoats and sent him toward the border to gather Tory help for the army. Ferguson's search in the next weeks did nothing but convince him that the countryside was teeming with American patriots. Daily, they sniped away at his men, dropping them one by one with deadly accurate musket fire.

Ferguson at last had to take refuge on the steep slopes of Kings Mountain, which dominated the border dividing the Carolinas. There, he was sure he could hold out against the sharpshooters until Cornwallis arrived. He was mistaken. A band of Kentuckians, firing from behind the rocks on the mountain, crawled toward his position on October 7, methodically thinning his ranks with their unerring marksmanship. Faced with certain defeat, Ferguson then made another mistake—one that cost him his life. Rather than surrendering, he ordered a bayonet charge against the Kentuckians in an attempt to drive

Francis Marion and Thomas Sumter

Marion and Sumter harassed the redcoat troops throughout the British campaign in the southern states.

Because of his excellent fighting in the southern swamplands, Marion was known as the "Swamp Fox." The famous South Carolina fort that was the site of the Civil War's first shots was named for Sumter.

Marion's deeds were celebrated in song, as this sheet music cover shows.

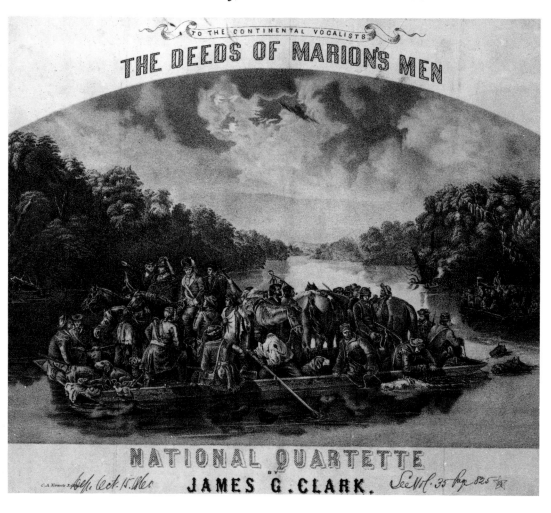

them off, only to see his redcoated ranks shredded to pieces by the well-concealed musketmen. Ferguson himself was fatally struck. With his death, his remaining men surrendered.

When news of Ferguson's fate reached Cornwallis, he retreated a distance and settled his men into camp for several weeks. General Nathanael Greene, who was given the southern command by Washington after Gates's shameful defeat at Camden, used the time to move an army into South Carolina and divide it into two units, one to either side of Cornwallis. The Britisher attempted to sabotage this plot by sending troops under Banastre Tarleton against one of the units. They fought at Cowpens, with the redcoats suffering a devastating defeat.

Now, with Greene harassing him every step of the way, Cornwallis moved into North Carolina as 1781 dawned. At Guilford Courthouse on March 15, he met Greene in a battle that ended in a draw. Then, with the Americans still pursuing, aided by Francis Marion's and Thomas Sumter's guerrilla fighters, Cornwallis marched on to Virginia.

On arriving, like Ferguson on Kings Mountain, Cornwallis was to make a fatal mistake. It would not cost him his life; rather, it would cost him the war.

CHAPTER 8

Yorktown

Cornwallis swept into Virginia in the spring of 1781. He spent the next months working his way up the state. Then he made his fatal mistake. Tired of the fighting and marching, he moved his troops to Yorktown, a small tobacco-trading port on a peninsula that jutted out into Chesapeake Bay. In so doing, he put his back to the water and made escape difficult—if not impossible—should the Americans now seal off the peninsula on its land and bay sides.

Cornwallis was aware of this danger when he settled his 7,000 British and Hessian troops in the little town in August. He was willing to take the risk because he was counting on General Clinton sending him reinforcements by sea from New York City. Once he was reinforced and had a number of warships at hand, he would escape the peninsula and carry on the war.

But Clinton was slow in sending the needed reinforcements. Further, Britain no longer had as many ships as before to assign to the American problem. Spain and Holland, in 1779 and 1780 respectively, had joined France

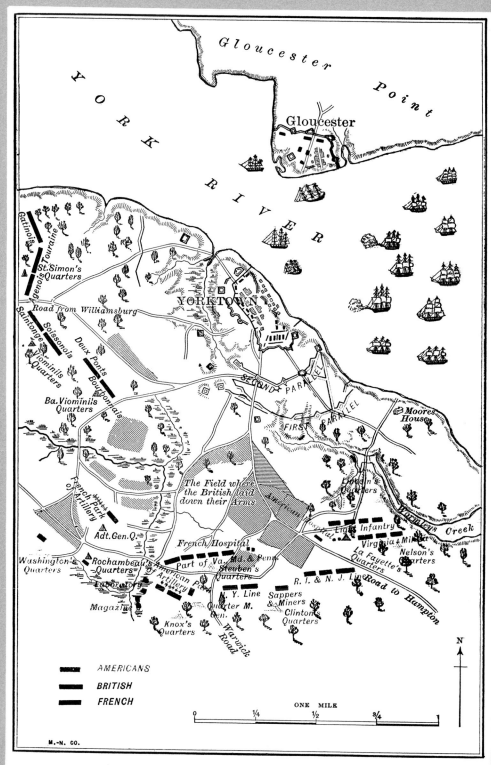

The siege of Yorktown. When French ships sailed up the York River, they blocked the only escape route for the British.

in opposing England in the Revolutionary War. Many British ships were staying close to home to defend Britain against a possible invasion by French and Spanish fleets.

All this gave Washington (who was delighted at the news of what Cornwallis had done) the time he needed to close the trap that the Britisher had set for himself. He sent orders to the Marquis de Lafayette, who had been fighting Cornwallis in Virginia, to seal off the neck of the peninsula and stop any enemy attempt at an overland break to freedom. Then he led his army on a 300-mile (483-kilometer) march from New York state into Virginia. Thrusting south at the same time, on Washington's orders, were French troops that had been encamped in Rhode Island. They were commanded by Count de Rochambeau. Altogether, the American and French marchers numbered some 16,000 men.

As Washington was moving south, a fleet of twenty-eight French warships carrying 3,000 troops was sailing into Chesapeake Bay. Commanded by Admiral Count de Grasse, the fleet had been in the Caribbean Sea and had immediately swung north on receiving instructions to meet Washington at Yorktown.

Both the American-French army and the French warships reached the peninsula at approximately the same

General Henry Clinton

Clinton took command of the British troops in America after General Howe captured Philadelphia. He was later slow in sending reinforcements to Cornwallis at Yorktown. It was well known that he and Cornwallis disliked each other. When Clinton was young, his father served as governor of the New York colony.

time. The British were now hopelessly trapped on all sides as Washington spread his troops out in a semicircle across the neck of the peninsula. It was now October and the scene was set for what would be the final major action of war.

YORKTOWN UNDER SIEGE

The siege of Yorktown opened on October 9, 1781, with a heavy artillery bombardment. In the next days, with the roar of their cannons deafening them, Washington's forces attacked and overran the first of the British fortifications that Cornwallis had built in front of the town. Its capture enabled the attackers to move their artillery closer to their targets so that the bombardment became ever more devastating. By mid-month, the British were crouching under a continuous rain of cannon balls.

And, by mid-month, Cornwallis fully realized that his situation was hopeless; that help from Clinton in New York would never arrive in time to be of help—if, indeed, it ever arrived at all (actually, a rescue force was just then departing New York City). A few days later, on October 18, he knew the end had come. More than one hundred American guns unleashed a deadly bombardment. One British gun emplacement after another was reduced to a smoldering ruin. At last, the remaining guns fell silent; their ammunition was gone. Admitting that he could do nothing but surrender, General Cornwallis sent a drummer boy up to a parapet to beat out the call for a parley with the enemy. The American and French troops could not hear him in the midst of their cannon fire. But they could see his red coat. They understood. Their gunfire dwindled away to silence.

[93]

General Charles Cornwallis

Cornwallis thought that he had taken all the fight out of Washington when he pursued the Americans through New Jersey to Pennsylvania. He left his troops on the banks of the Delaware River and went to New York City, only to hurry back to them after Washington's victory at Trenton. He was appointed Governor General of India in the late 1780s. While there, he introduced land reforms, developed a new criminal code, and established a new court system.

A British officer now appeared on the parapet. An American officer came forward, blindfolded him, and led him to the American lines. The Britisher explained that Cornwallis was ready to surrender and was asking for twenty-four hours to arrange the terms of the surrender. Washington granted him two hours and stated the terms that the Americans would accept. The officer nodded and returned to Yorktown.

It was not until the next day, however, that the terms were finally arranged. They called for Cornwallis to surrender all his arms and military equipment. Officers, however, were to be allowed to keep their sidearms and were to be sent home or to some area still in British hands. Cornwallis's soldiers were to become prisoners of war. All that remained was the actual ceremony of surrender.

OCTOBER 19, 1781

That ceremony took place at 2:00 P.M. on October 19. The music of fife and drum filled the warmish air as the American and French armies marched across battle-torn fields to take up positions on either side of the road that ran for two miles from Yorktown to the field where Cornwallis's troops would lay down their arms. The two armies stood facing each other in silence. The French were resplendent in their white uniforms. In comparison, the Americans, whose Congress—despite the French financial aid—had not the money to clothe them properly, looked an untidy lot in their tattered homespun, with a patched and frayed Continental uniform showing here and there. Only Washington and those officers who could afford to buy their own uniforms were to be seen in the army's blue and buff outfits.

[95]

Washington sat astride a bay horse in the field at the far end of his troops. Mounted directly opposite him was the French army's Count de Rochambeau. They soon heard new music in the distance. It heralded the arrival of Cornwallis's British and Hessian troops, who now marched down the road between the watching Americans and Frenchmen. The Hessians marched silently, with backs straight. But the redcoats were openly disgusted at losing to the raw-boned Americans and the hated French. Some were weeping. Some were drunk.

The surrender at Yorktown. The French are on the left and the Americans on the right.

At their head rode General Charles O'Hara, deputy commander under Cornwallis. Cornwallis had conveniently "fallen ill" that morning and had passed to his deputy the humiliating task of handing over the sword of surrender. When he reached the point where Washington and Rochambeau sat mounted opposite each other, O'Hara seemed confused, as if not knowing which man to approach. He decided on Rochambeau and rode over to him, ready to unsheath his sword.

Rochambeau shook his head and glanced in Washington's direction. O'Hara flushed at his error and swung about to the American. Washington greeted him courteously and asked why General Cornwallis was not present. When he heard the answer, he turned in his saddle and called for General Benjamin Lincoln, the officer who had tried so valiantly to retake Savannah. On the spot, he appointed Lincoln as *his* deputy. Since a deputy was presenting the sword of surrender, a deputy would receive it.

Once O'Hara's sword had passed to Lincoln, the shouted order went out for the enemy soldiers to lay down their arms. The Hessians stacked their muskets neatly. But many of the redcoats threw down their guns with such force that they seemed to be trying to break them. Then the defeated troops, no longer looking like a trim and experienced army, turned and trudged silently back to Yorktown.

The surrender ceremony had taken no more than a few moments. It had been simple. It had been marred by a lapse in military protocol on O'Hara's part. It had featured no inspiring speeches by the victors. But none of that mattered. What mattered was that the last great battle of the American War of Independence had been fought.

Epilogue: Victory and Independence

Many Americans mistakenly think that the surrender at Yorktown marked the close of the Revolutionary War. Actually, the conflict did not end until 1783 when, after long negotiations with three American envoys (Benjamin Franklin, John Adams, and John Jay) the British signed the Treaty of Paris. In the interim there was more fighting, but it was not of the magnitude that had been seen before. Much of it was waged between Tories and Patriots.

The Yorktown surrender was important because it opened the way to the peace negotiations. Both sides were exhausted by the fighting and eager for an honorable peace.

Britain seemed to be the more eager of the two. It was beset by troubles with France and Spain. Its Parliament was now led by men who were sympathetic to the American cause, strongly opposed King George's desire to continue the war, and willing to recognize America's independence.

Americans have often marveled at the fact that our country managed to win the war. The infant country never

Benjamin Franklin, John Adams, and John Jay

The three American participants in the negotiations that led to the Treaty of Paris all served their country not only during but after the revolution. Both Franklin and Adams helped to write and then signed the Declaration of Independence. Franklin, as America's first minister to France, was instrumental in arranging French support of the revolution. In the post-war years, he served for three years as the president of the executive council of Pennsylvania; he was in his eighties at the time. Adams went on to become America's second president. Jay was appointed the first chief justice of the United States Supreme Court.

The Treaty of Paris officially ended the war. This view of the signing in 1782 shows John Jay and Benjamin Franklin standing, and John Adams seated holding the document.

had enough money to spend on the fighting. Dissention raged between Tories and Patriots at all times. Washington's troops were far outnumbered by their British opponents, who were recognized as among the finest troops in the world. Many of the American soldiers abandoned Washington at times—some because they thought the war lost, some because their terms of enlistment were up, and some (farmers who often returned later) because they had to go home and help their families at harvest time.

Though America faced many disadvantages, it also brought a number of advantages to the conflict. One was Washington's brilliant leadership, a leadership that, for instance, staggered the Hessians at Trenton. Another was the Patriots' use of Indian tactics (guerrilla tactics) that the British soldiers, who were accustomed to battles in open fields, found hard to handle. Further, the Americans, especially those from farms and the backwoods, were deadly marksmen.

Then there was the fact that the British generals in America took their orders from the government in London. The time that was needed to send those orders—and supplies and reinforcements—out to the New World slowed the speed at which the redcoat forces could conduct the war. On top of all else was the fact that, on more than one occasion, the British generals did not follow up immediately on attacks that had put the Americans in retreat. Howe's slowness in attacking Washington after the battle of Brooklyn Heights, when he had the chance to destroy the American army, stands as a prime example of the opportunities that were lost by hesitant British generalship.

Finally, there was one overwhelming advantage held by the Americans who loyally stayed with Washington throughout the long years of fighting. It was their ruggedness and their determination to win. These were the factors that made it possible for the newborn United States to survive the ordeal of its birth and begin its march to the position it holds in the world today.

Bibliography

Bailey, Thomas A. *The American Pageant: A History of the Republic.* Boston: D.C. Heath, 1956.

Carruth, Gorton. *The Encyclopedia of American Facts and Dates.* 9th edition. New York: HarperCollins, 1993.

Commager, Henry Steele, and Richard B. Morris, editors. *The Spirit of 'Seventy-Six.* Indianapolis: Bobbs-Merrill, 1958.

Freeman, Douglas S. *George Washington.* Volumes 3, 4, and 5. New York: Scribner, 1948.

Garraty, John A. *1001 Things Everyone Should Know About American History.* New York: Doubleday, 1989.

Garraty, John A. and Peter Gay, editors. *The Columbia History of the World.* New York: Harper & Row, 1972.

Hall, John Whitney, general editor. *History of the World.* Volume 2. *The Renaissance to World War II.* Greenwich, Connecticut: Bison Books, 1988.

Hart, Michael H. *The 100: A Ranking of the Most Influential Persons in History* (chapters on George Washington, Thomas Jefferson, and Benjamin Franklin). New York: Hart, 1978.

Hicks, John D. *A Short History of American Democracy.* Boston: Houghton Mifflin, 1949.

Lancaster, Bruce. *From Lexington to Liberty*. New York: Double-day, 1955.

———. *The American Heritage Book of the Revolution*. New York: Simon & Schuster, 1958.

Leckie, Robert. *The Wars of America*. Volume 1: From *1600* to *1900*. New York: HarperCollins, 1992.

Miller, John C. *Triumph of Freedom, 1775–1783*. Boston: Little, Brown, 1948.

Nevins, Allan, and Henry Steele Commager. *A Short History of the United States*. Boston: Little, Brown, 1942.

Pratt, Fletcher. *The Battles That Changed History*. New York: Doubleday, 1956.

Roberts, J. M. *History of the World*. New York: Oxford University Press, 1993.

Stokesbury, James L. *A Short History of the American Revolution*. New York: William Morrow, 1991.

Ward, Christopher. *The War of the Revolution*. New York: Macmillan, 1953.

Index